NIDO R. QUBEIN | NICK NANTON | JW DICKS

HOW SUCCESSFUL PEOPLE THINK

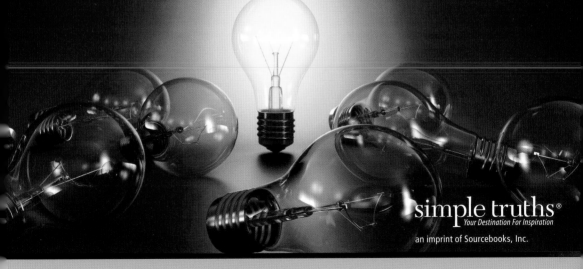

simple truths®
Your Destination For Inspiration

an imprint of Sourcebooks, Inc.

Moving from Ordinary to Extraordinary

Editing by: Alice Patenaude

Photo Credits
Cover: front, vasabii/Shutterstock; back, Lynn Harker/Sourcebooks
Internals: page 1, vasabii/Shutterstock; page 8, Lynn Harker/Sourcebooks; page 23, Isaiah Johnson/Sourcebooks; page 25, KsushaArt/Shutterstock; page 29, rozbyshaka/Shutterstock; page 31, Kotkoa/Shutterstock; page 33, Isaiah Johnson/Sourcebooks; pages 34–35, peepo/iStock; page 37, lisegagne/iStock; page 39, browndogstudios/iStock; page 44, adamkaz/iStock; page 47, stevecoleimages/iStock; page 48, sheelamohanachandran2010/Shutterstock; page 50, gehringj/iStock; page 59, Isaiah Johnson/Sourcebooks; pages 60–61, NickS/iStock; page 63, red rose/Shutterstock; page 64, 41/Shutterstock; page 66–67, caracterdesign/iStock; page 71, Romolo Tavani/Shutterstock; page 72, best works/Shutterstock; page 74, dip/Shutterstock; page 75, file404/Shutterstock; page 77, ventdusud/Shutterstock; page 84, paulprescott72/Shutterstock; pages 86–87, Zoom Team/Shutterstock.

Published by Simple Truths, an imprint of Sourcebooks, Inc.
P.O. Box 4410, Naperville, Illinois 60567-4410
(630) 961-3900
Fax: (630) 961-2168
www.sourcebooks.com

Printed and bound in China.
PP 10 9 8 7 6 5 4 3

TABLE OF CONTENTS

INTRODUCTION

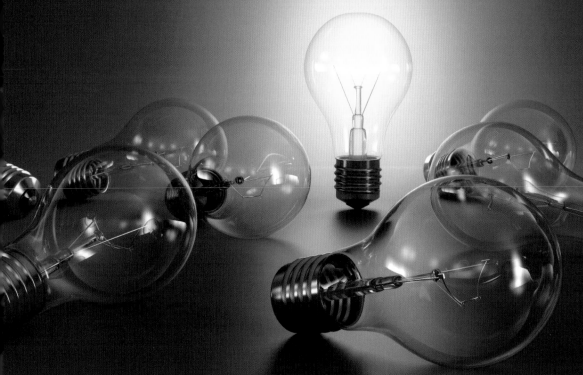

"Success is doing ordinary things extraordinarily well."

—JIM ROHN

Many of you may feel your everyday life never rises above the routine. You believe you're living a so-called "normal" life—and nothing more. But, as the Bible says, we reap what we sow. Often, we obtain only ordinary results because we approach life in an ordinary manner.

However, when we lose that *ordinary* mind-set—and, instead, take on the mantle of the *extraordinary*—it's truly amazing how much we can improve the lives of those around us and how many hidden rewards we can uncover for ourselves.

It's how successful people think. They always want to transform the ordinary to the extraordinary. You, too, can enhance any personal or business relationship by becoming extraordinary, but only if you are committed to it, no matter what your current role is in life.

For example, let's say you have a menial and ultimately unsatisfying job. When you're in that position, you may be tempted, to "phone it in"—to do what you have to do to get through the day and get back home—and, in the meantime, daydream about your *real* aspirations in life.

In other words, do what's required and nothing more. Do an "ordinary" job. No one is expecting more, right?

Well, *you* should!

Those ordinary jobs can become learning opportunities and extraordinary stepping stones to the life of your dreams. Here are a few folks who *did* expect more—and who made sure they got it:

> **Simon Cowell,** multimillionaire music mogul of *American Idol* and *The X Factor* fame, began his career in the EMI records mailroom.

Wally Amos, the founder of Famous Amos cookies, started in the William Morris Agency's mailroom and later became the first black talent agent in their history. He made his fortune by sending out his chocolate chip wonders to showbiz greats who then backed his amazingly successful cookie company.

Helen Gurley Brown began her career as a secretary at an ad agency. She became one of the highest-paid ad copywriters in the country, wrote a bestseller, and took over *Cosmopolitan,* a failing magazine, turning it into a decades-long success story.

Barry Diller, the former head of Paramount Pictures, also started out in the William Morris Agency mailroom. He now serves as chairman of Expedia, Inc., and IAC/InterActiveCorp and has an estimated net worth of more than two billion dollars.

These successful people saw extraordinary opportunity in *very* ordinary positions. By approaching lower-level positions that others took for granted with the right mind-set, they positioned themselves for stellar success.

What it all comes down to is this:

When you transform the ordinary to the extraordinary, you create benefits for everyone involved, including yourself.

When you give your best to every situation—when you make your strongest effort, even when nothing is promised in return—you improve the world and reap greater personal rewards, especially over the long run.

In this book, we're going to look closely at how successful people routinely move from ordinary to extraordinary and how you can do that in almost every aspect of life. We'll also examine how to attain the extraordinary *mind-set* that all great achievers possess—to always deliver the most value possible.

When you move from ordinary to extraordinary, everyone wins. The result is abundance—the more good you create in the world, the more of it you will experience!

CHAPTER 1

ADDING VALUE:
THE ESSENCE OF THE EXTRAORDINARY

"Price is what you pay. Value is what you get."
—WARREN BUFFETT

One word above all others drives sales when describing products on the home shopping channels: *value.* That word suggests you're getting a product that delivers more than its price would suggest.

Who doesn't love that? Who doesn't want to get *more* from a transaction than they expect? Who doesn't look forward to dealing with a person who they *know* will deliver that kind of experience?

Increasing value is the very essence of moving from ordinary to extraordinary. Here are three people who could never conceive doing anything less...

"Be a yardstick of quality. Some people aren't used to an environment where excellence is expected."

—Steve Jobs

Steve Jobs was a visionary who understood, perhaps more than any other CEO, how value is linked to realizing extraordinary results. He could charge more for his products because they were innovative, exciting, and did things that his competitors' products didn't. His customers were happy to pay more—and enthusiastic about what product Apple would roll out next.

Jeff Bezos, founder of Amazon.com, brought the extraordinary to the ordinary shopping experience. He changed retail forever by seeing the selling power of the Internet before anyone else—gathering everything anyone could want under one virtual banner and putting those products in his customers' hands with just one click.

"There are two kinds of companies: those that work to try to charge more and those that work to charge less. We will be the second."

—*Jeff Bezos*

"Use what you have to run toward your best—that's how I now live my life."

—*Oprah Winfrey*

Oprah Winfrey transformed the too-often ordinary role of being a television personality. She added value to the talk show arena with her piercing insight and incredible empathy and, in the process, inspired her audiences around the world to do and live better.

Value is an intangible concept, but it has many tangible aspects. For value to be recognized, it must possess some or all of these qualities:

VISIBILITY: If you can't perceive added value, you can't appreciate it.

ALIGNMENT: Value must be aligned within the goals and strategies of what you are trying to achieve.

LEADERSHIP: Innovation and excellence must be sought after by leaders who will raise the bar when it comes to value.

UNDERSTANDING: You must understand what others truly value before you can deliver it.

ENHANCEMENT: Value, by definition, implies an improvement over the mundane. If you supply what everyone else is supplying, you don't stand out.

VALUE is always in the eye of the beholder. Put these five elements in play and you'll see an extraordinary sparkle in the recipient's eye.

CREATING AN EXTRAORDINARY YOU

"You will be as much value to others as you have been to yourself."

—MARCUS TULLIUS CICERO

Demosthenes **was one of the greatest orators of ancient Greece. And yet, this iconic statesman, still renowned over two thousand years later, was born with a seemingly insurmountable speech defect. How did he overcome it? Legend has it he spoke for hours on end with pebbles in his mouth.**

In other words, Demosthenes was not born great. *He made himself great.*

To move from ordinary to extraordinary, we must first find ways to make *ourselves* extraordinary. The more value we create in ourselves, the more value we can offer the world—and the more personal rewards we will reap.

Here are **THREE KEY WAYS** to become more than you are... and perhaps more than you ever thought possible.

1. OVERCOME LIMITATIONS

Thomas Edison, Henry Ford, Ted Turner, and **Richard Branson** all struggled in school because they were dyslexic. But you could say that dyslexia was almost a gift, because it motivated all four of these amazing men to develop strong wills and to think outside the box. They were *forced* to create more powerful versions of themselves—and achieved greatness because of it. In the words of another famous dyslexic, **Tom Cruise**: *"I'd gotten to where I was operating on the force of sheer will."*

Always grow beyond what's holding you back...and continue to move forward.

2. ACQUIRE NEW KNOWLEDGE AND SKILLS

If it weren't for **Steve Jobs**, we might not have the multitude of computer fonts that are at our disposal today. Why? Because his unquenchable desire to learn led him to audit random college classes, one of which happened to be in calligraphy, even though Jobs never thought it would have any practical application in his life…until he began developing his breakthrough Macintosh computer. In his words:

"It was the first computer with beautiful typography. If I had never dropped in on that single course in college, the Mac would have never had multiple typefaces or proportionally spaced fonts. And since Windows just copied the Mac, it's likely that no personal computer would have them."

Taking on new knowledge and skills opens doors to the unexpected achievement of the extraordinary.

3. IMPROVE ON EXISTING ABILITIES AND TALENTS

Truly successful people never stop growing and improving. Facebook CEO **Mark Zuckerberg** undertakes a new and challenging self-improvement task every year, such as learning Mandarin Chinese or forcing himself to talk to one new person outside of Facebook every day. He relates these annual assignments directly back to improving his CEO abilities:

"I think a lot of building something is just about kind of seeing things through. And so I try to pick things that are going to be hard for me to do."

There are many talented people in the world. But there are far fewer *successful* talented people.

No matter what rung you're clutching on life's ladder, there is always another above you to reach for. The further you elevate yourself, the more you will be looked up to...and the more influence you will have.

CHAPTER 3

PASSION: AN EXTRAORDINARY FUEL

"When it becomes clear that no one else shares your level of passion, you are where you belong."

—PLACIDO DOMINGO

Just as there's a difference between the ordinary and the extraordinary, there is a difference between doing something...and *wanting* to do something.

Between going through the motions...and going the extra mile.

Between working...and working it.

The difference is **passion**. And all successful people possess it.

Jimi Hendrix understood passion. He practiced the guitar until his fingers bled. He even learned to play his beloved instrument with his teeth. *"Music is my religion,"* he famously said— because he couldn't imagine doing anything else.

Passion pushes us forward. It makes us excited to achieve and motivates us to work harder and longer than others. Passion inspires us to look for every single possible way to do what we do *better.*

Our minds may guide us in creating plans to achieve, but our hearts inspire us to fulfill those plans.

Unfortunately, it's all too easy to lose our passion. Overwhelming difficulties cause us to question it. Daily routine dilutes it. Repeated setbacks can drain it.

But passion can be reclaimed.

Enthusiasm can be rekindled.

Make your fire burn brighter

than ever before by…

1. KEEPING THE END IN SIGHT

When a climbing expedition attempts to scale Mount Everest, it is confronted with scores of life-threatening possibilities: the deadly effects of high winds and severe cold, the tragedy that could result from a simple slip or fall, or the alarming lack of oxygen at extremely high altitudes. In order to mentally succeed, the climbers must continually visualize one image—*the peak of the mountain*. It's the reason *why* they're risking everything.

*Always keep your "**why**" in mind.*

Remind yourself of your end goals when difficulties present themselves or the road suddenly appears longer than you imagined. Picture them. Even find visual representations of them to contemplate.

See your future, and you'll achieve more in the present.

"Visualize this thing that you want. See it, feel it, believe in it. Make your mental blueprint, and begin to build."

—*Robert Collier*

2. PERCEIVING CHALLENGES AS OPPORTUNITIES

The great Western movie director **John Ford** was once shooting a scene with a cavalry riding through the middle of his favorite location, Monument Valley, a Navajo Nation tribal park. The cinematographer, Winton Hoch, saw storm clouds building and announced they had to stop filming because the shot would be too dark. Ford saw stunning lightning strikes in the distance and wanted Hoch to keep shooting. Hoch did, but under protest.

The resulting footage was so amazing that the reluctant cinematographer won the Academy Award for his work on *She Wore a Yellow Ribbon*.

What seems to be an obstacle can often be an opportunity to go in a better and more rewarding direction. We only need to stop complaining and start looking at things with fresh eyes. At the very worst, problems require us to become smarter, more resourceful, and more determined.

Difficulties make us better—

as long as we don't walk away from them.

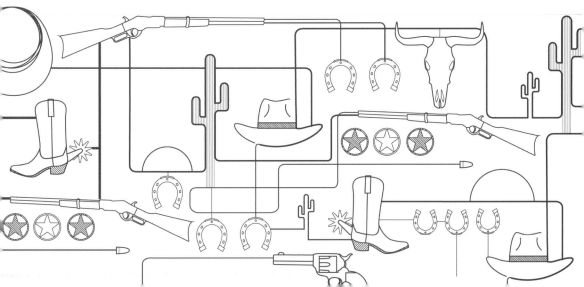

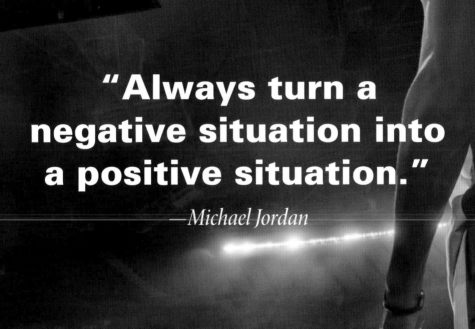

"Always turn a negative situation into a positive situation."

—*Michael Jordan*

3. RESTING AND RECHARGING

Burn out. That's what happens when you spin around in circles, 24–7, trying to get task after task done without bothering to take a break. When you don't let up, you fall down. You lose perspective, your priorities fall apart, and your life satisfaction fades.

When you allow space in your work routine for your brain to relax and unwind, your unconscious will go to work, giving you more than you ever dreamed possible.

LITERALLY.

Paul McCartney dreamed the tune for the Beatles classic "Yesterday." James Cameron dreamed the prototype for his movie smash *The Terminator.* And Albert Einstein dreamed the earliest version of his theory of relativity.

Allow yourself time to do nothing. You'll gain new energy to do more in the long run.

"Your mind will
answer most questions
if you learn to relax and wait
for the answer."

—*William S. Burroughs*

"People often say
that motivation
doesn't last.
Well, neither does
bathing—that's why
we recommend
it daily."

—Zig Ziglar

Tap into your passion.
When it begins to run dry,
drill for more.

CHAPTER 4

RELATIONSHIPS: CREATING EXTRAORDINARY BONDS

"The meeting of two personalities is like the contact of two chemical substances: if there is any reaction, both are transformed."

—CARL JUNG

We never truly accomplish anything by ourselves.

Wilbur Wright may have built the first airplane, but it was Orville who flew it.

Steve Jobs may have ended up as the sole face of Apple, but it was the partner he founded the company with, Steve Wozniak, who built the first Apple computer.

And Thomas Edison may get all the credit for inventing the phonograph, but it was John Kruesi, Edison's employee who made all of twelve dollars a week, who actually found the way to turn the idea into reality.

The fact is that strong, positive relationships in business, and in life, yield extraordinary results. According to **Keith Ferrazzi**, bestselling author and CEO of Ferrazzi Greenlight, a research institute and strategic consulting firm:

> *"Our research shows that the number-one predictive element of an individual's success is the number, the quality, and the depth of social capital—the personal relationships among those that they do business with."*

Why does this hold true? Because none of us possess *all* the skills, knowledge, or connections we need to reach our most cherished goals. When we make the time to build great relationships with great people, we create a limitless pool of resources that we can tap into as needed.

And we also feel the joy of helping people achieve more when we are able to contribute to another person's goals.

Extraordinary relationships are possible when the connection is *authentic.* When we genuinely feel a connection with others, we *want* to engage with them.

Bill Hewlett and Dave Packard were fellow Stanford students who shared an insatiable curiosity as well as a drive to achieve. Together, they founded a technology dynasty because they shared the same ambition. A few decades later, Stanford classmates Jerry Yang and David Filo shared a similar connection and enjoyed similar results— as the founders of Yahoo!

Would any of the individuals in these two-man teams have achieved as much on their own? Most likely not. A powerful relationship is almost always an example of the whole being greater than the sum of its parts.

"A winning effort begins with preparation."

—Joe Gibbs

Extraordinary relationships are possible when we ***choose wisely.***

Think of those individuals who pick their spouses primarily on the basis of how much money they have or how attractive they are. Think of how often those relationships end in disaster.

When coach **Herb Brooks** was putting together the U.S. hockey team for the 1980 Olympics, he told his assistant he wasn't looking for the *best* players—he was looking for the *right* players. That team famously beat the odds-on favorite Soviet team in one of the biggest upsets in sports history, as portrayed in the movie *Miracle on Ice*.

Personal chemistry and character dictate the strength and success of a relationship. The *right* connection brings the right results.

Likewise, the *wrong* connection can bring about never-ending conflict and disappointment. When you choose to work with those who cheat others, they will eventually cheat you. When you choose to work with angry and vindictive personalities, they will eventually focus their wrath on you.

As Jim Rohn once said, *"You are the average of the five people you spend the most time with."* Spend your time with uplifting and productive people.

"I mean, if the relationship can't survive the long term, why on earth would it be worth my time and energy for the short term?"

—*Nicholas Sparks*

"To add value to others, one must first value others."

—*John C. Maxwell*

Finally, extraordinary relationships are possible when each person has **something to offer.**

None of us is perfect, and we consciously or unconsciously look to associate with those who can "fill in our blanks." If we have grand ideas but no hands-on abilities, we look for those who can bring those ideas to life. If we're sloppy and unorganized, we look for those who can help us bring order into our lives. If we lack access to the gatekeepers who could help our progress, we look for those who have powerful networks.

There's nothing wrong with getting our needs met—as long as we also make an effort to meet the other person's as well. A one-sided relationship is easily tipped over, while a balanced one has an enduring strength and stability that pays long-term dividends.

Give back what you receive in every relationship. Honor the other person and you will also be recognized. Value exchanged creates a bond that is hard to break.

Remember that the range and scope of human cooperation exceeds that of every other species on earth—that's why we've achieved so much. Our individual gifts, when unified, truly become an extraordinary force.

CHAPTER 5

DELIVERING THE EXTRAORDINARY

"No student ever attains very eminent success by simply doing what is required of him: it is the amount and excellence of what is over and above the required, that determines the greatness of ultimate distinction."

—CHARLES KENDALL ADAMS

A businessman was staying at the Ritz-Carlton on St. Thomas. He decided to try out a paddleboard for the first time and ended up losing his balance, as well as his sunglasses, when he plunged into the water.

Later that day, when he was strolling through the grounds, a hotel staff member approached him and asked, "Did you lose your sunglasses?" The staffer then handed the astonished guest the very pair he thought was lost at the bottom of the sea.

How was this miracle accomplished?

When the guest returned his paddleboard to the hotel's rental center, the clerk noticed he was missing his sunglasses. He said nothing to the man and, instead, set up a snorkeling expedition to retrieve the Ray-Bans.

It was no miracle. It was simply paying attention to detail and **acting on it**.

Delivering the extraordinary and finding success begins with one simple question:

"How can I do it better?"

If you don't have this question in the back of your mind as you go through your day, you will almost certainly find the extraordinary out of your reach.

Horst Schulze, the legendary founder of the Ritz-Carlton Hotel Company, which is rightly revered for their customer service, defined their sky-high standard as the "fulfillment of unexpressed wishes and needs." Consider these methods of delivering the extraordinary in every aspect of your life:

1. CREATE THE "WOW"

A business consultant heading back to New York City had missed lunch and was facing a two-and-a-half-hour flight without food. As a joke, he tweeted to his favorite steak house before takeoff: "Hey, @Mortons, can you meet me at Newark airport with a porterhouse when I land in two hours? K, thanks. :)"

When he landed, he was met by a waiter in a tuxedo carrying a full steak dinner, complete with silverware and a napkin.

During that two-and-a-half-hour flight, someone at the restaurant had to see the tweet, get the food prepared, track down the man's flight information, and drive the dinner the twenty-five miles or so to the airport to meet him.

That's a definite WOW.

Whether you're proposing to a special someone on a sports stadium Jumbotron screen or delivering a work report in half the allotted time with twice the quality, you're delivering an experience that will impress the recipient in an extraordinary way.

The result? That person will talk about you to everyone around them, and those people will talk about you to everyone they know.

A moment of WOW carries echoes that travel a huge distance. A moment of WOW can create lasting loyalty that stands the test of time.

"Here is a simple but powerful rule: always give people more than what they expect to get."

—Nelson Boswell

2. DON'T DISAPPOINT

A **WOW** moment creates impactful word of mouth, but so does a negative experience. Perhaps even more so.

When an airline's baggage handler broke a passenger's custom-made guitar, the passenger created a YouTube video bad-mouthing the company that ended up getting two million views. And millions is what it cost the airline. Analysts said the video drove down the airline's stock 10 percent, costing them *$180 million* in value.

All because of a damaged guitar.

Correction. All because of the airline's initial *response* to a damaged guitar.

Prior to creating the video, the guitar player called the company countless times and spent $1,200 of his own money to repair the instrument. When he received no compensation, he made his case to YouTube.

To be honest, we all know accidents happen. Things go wrong. We all sometimes fail to deliver what is promised.

But we also have the power to turn a bad situation into a great one—if we act quickly to rectify what's gone wrong.

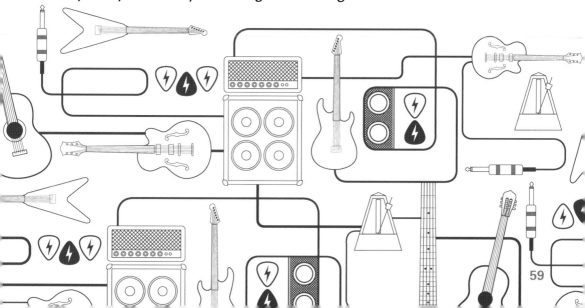

"Customers don't expect you to be perfect. They do expect you to fix things when they go wrong."

—*Donald Porter, vice president, British Airways*

3. ACKNOWLEDGE EMOTIONS

There is nothing stronger than an emotional bond. When you react to someone's feelings in a proactive way, you create an extraordinary connection they will cherish.

The online shoe retailer Zappos, another company renowned for its exemplary service, understands this important concept. Here's the proof:

A customer's mother was having medical problems that affected her feet and she suddenly wasn't able to wear any of her existing shoes. The daughter ordered six pairs of shoes, hoping some of them might do the trick. When the mom called to ask how to return the shoes that didn't work, she told the company rep why she had to try so many different ones.

Two days later, Zappos sent the mother a huge bouquet of flowers, wishing her a speedy recovery, and upgraded her to a Zappos VIP member, where she received free and fast shipping on all orders.

Contrast that with the cell phone company who kept charging a woman for her father's account—three months after he had passed away, and even after she had sent the company his death certificate. That company's rep said he couldn't do anything about it and she heard him laugh as he hung up the phone.

"I've learned that people will forget what you said, people will forget what you did, but people will never forget how you made them feel."

—*Maya Angelou*

No matter how high your position might be, see yourself as a servant. See yourself as someone who can deliver good, even great, work to those around you. It's the attitude of every extraordinary person.

"Good leaders must first become good servants."

—Robert K. Greenleaf

CHAPTER 6

EXTRAORDINARY GOALS, EXTRAORDINARY RESULTS

"It's kind of fun to do the impossible."
—WALT DISNEY

Bill Gates and Paul Allen were childhood friends who eventually founded one of the great technology companies of our time—Microsoft. That wasn't an accident.

When Gates was thirteen years old, he obsessively read *Fortune* magazine. One day, he turned to Allen and said, "What do you think it's like to run a Fortune 500 company?" It was a moment that Allen never forgot because it indicated the incredibly high aspirations Gates already had for his future.

Rare is the individual who moves from ordinary to extraordinary without first having extraordinary ambitions. Call it the law of attraction, if you will, but it takes a strong and determined mind-set, focused on lofty and so-called "unrealistic" goals to attain great results.

When someone makes an incredible breakthrough in any field, from sports to technology, it first seems like magic. That "magic" is the result of a will to succeed and the belief that all things are possible.

If you don't believe in the extraordinary, you cannot achieve it.

During his first year in office, President **John F. Kennedy** stated that America would put a man on the moon by the end of the decade. At the time, it seemed as though the Russian space program had an insurmountable lead and the technology required for a lunar landing was still far in the future. Nevertheless, JFK inspired the nation with his words—and the motivation and commitment necessary to succeed followed.

Eight years later, the Apollo 11 mission made history by executing the first manned moon landing.

"**Nothing can stop the man with the right mental attitude from achieving his goal; nothing on earth can help the man with the wrong mental attitude.**"

—Thomas Jefferson

Attitude, of course, only provides the determination and motivation to achieve. Mind-set must be matched with action that will take us closer to our dreams.

Planning is essential. **Bill Gates** did not expect to just stumble into the role of CEO of a Fortune 500 company; he knew he needed a revolutionary product upon which he could begin to build his empire. A large long-term goal is attained by reaching a series of logical short-term goals along the way.

What must you do to move yourself toward your ultimate goals? What additional skills and knowledge do you need to obtain? Who do you know who has already reached a similar goal who you can reach out to for advice and help?

It's not enough to know where you're going. You need to know *how* to get there.

Perhaps the main reason many plans fail is because they're left open-ended. When **deadlines** are put in place and taken seriously, progress is inevitable. Make your plans realistic. Make them doable. But make them.

The more impossible your ambition seems, the more it needs to be anchored to a timeline. The less practical your goal seems, the more urgently you need to attach a concrete plan to it. That's how dreams are transformed into reality.

"Be able to meet any deadline, even if your work is done less well than it would be if you had all the time you would have preferred."

—*Marilyn vos Savant*

Two final ingredients are essential to achieving cherished goals—**focus** and **commitment.**

Before competing in the 2008 Olympics, Michael Phelps learned that his idol, swimmer Ian Thorpe, said Phelps was unlikely to win eight gold medals during the games. No athlete ever had. Phelps wrote those words down and pinned them up inside his locker. That summer, he won those record-setting eight gold medals.

When you keep your eye on the prize, you constantly visualize what you want to achieve and your mind and spirit lock into your desired destination.

That's when the real magic happens.

"The key to success is to focus our conscious mind on things we desire not things we fear."

—Brian Tracy

We can move from ordinary to extraordinary if we understand what it takes to achieve our goal—and take action to do what's required. Many great men and women were ridiculed for what they were determined to accomplish. And, in many cases, they had the last laugh.

FROM "IT COULDN'T BE DONE"

—Edgar Albert Guest

Somebody said that it couldn't be done

But he with a chuckle replied

That "maybe it couldn't," but he would be one

Who wouldn't say so till he'd tried.

So he buckled right in with the trace of a grin

On his face. If he worried he hid it.

He started to sing as he tackled the thing

That couldn't be done, and he did it!

CHAPTER 7

YOUR HIGHER VOICE:
BECOMING INTUITIVELY EXTRAORDINARY

"I've trusted the still, small voice of intuition my entire life. And the only time I've made mistakes is when I didn't listen…When you don't know what to do, do nothing. Get quiet so you can hear the still, small voice—your inner GPS guiding you to true North."

—OPRAH WINFREY

Being extraordinary is hard to define. Perhaps because it's often the result of forces we don't understand.

George Washington Carver, who discovered three hundred new uses for the peanut, and Luther Burbank, who developed over eight hundred new strains and varieties of plants, both claimed the same source for their innovative work—the plants themselves. Both claimed they "spoke" to the subjects of their work and that they learned everything they needed to know from them.

In Carver's words, *"Reading about nature is fine, but if a person walks in the woods and listens carefully, he can learn more than what is in books, for they speak with the voice of God."*

Carver and Burbank weren't the only scientists who relied more on intuition than facts. One of the greatest intellects of all time, Albert Einstein, believed that all great achievements start with intuitive knowledge. *"When I examine myself and my methods of thought, I come close to the conclusion that the gift of fantasy has meant more to me than any talent for absorbing absolute knowledge."*

To him, intuition was a sacred gift. And so it is with all successful people. Your intuition can help lead you from ordinary to extraordinary in your life—if you're willing to listen and willing to trust it.

But you must make room for it. Turn off the smartphone, put down the iPad, turn off the television, and find your inner voice. Open yourself up and let the wisdom you've been given innately guide you to the next step.

STAY POSITIVE. Focus on solutions, not problems. Look at what will work, not what didn't.

BE THANKFUL for what you have, not envious of what others possess. Appreciate what's good in your life and see how you can improve the bad.

STAY CENTERED. The world spins around us at a dizzying pace and we can easily lose our bearings if we go along for the ride.

LISTEN TO YOUR GUT. Don't let your fears and those of others overwhelm what you know to be true.

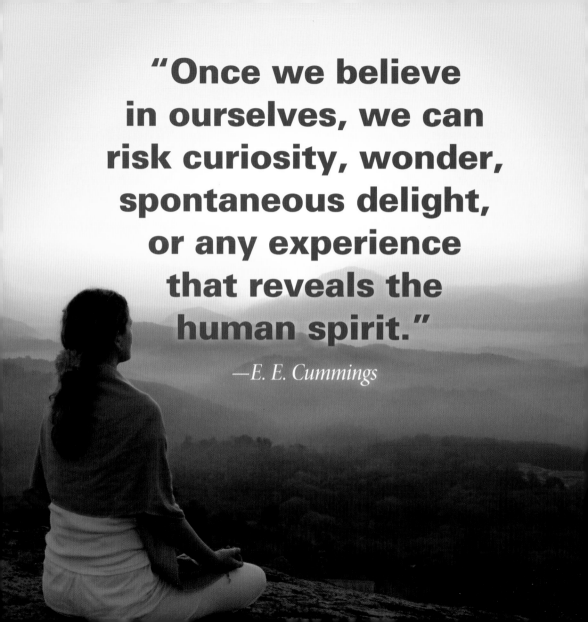

"Once we believe in ourselves, we can risk curiosity, wonder, spontaneous delight, or any experience that reveals the human spirit."

—E. E. Cummings

The extraordinary lives in us all. We only have to tap into what makes us unique to discover our true purpose. It's the calling card of the successful.

Nourish your spirit. Find your vision. Rise above the ordinary. And you will see the way to the fulfillment of your dreams.

"*Your time is limited, so don't waste it living someone else's life. Don't be trapped by dogma—which is living with the results of other people's thinking. Don't let the noise of other's opinions drown out your own inner voice. And most important, have the courage to follow your heart and intuition. They somehow already know what you truly want to become. Everything else is secondary.*"

—STEVE JOBS

ABOUT THE AUTHORS

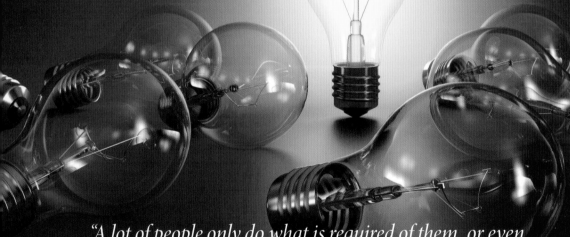

"A lot of people only do what is required of them, or even less; but achievers always do more than is required—and they do it with enthusiasm."

—DR. NIDO QUBEIN

NIDO R. QUBEIN

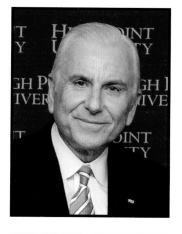

Dr. Nido R. Qubein came to the United States as a teenager with limited knowledge of English and only fifty dollars in his pocket. His inspiring life story is one filled with both adversity and abundance. It is through the lens of his life's journey that one appreciates his current role as an educator, philanthropist, and passionate advocate for the development of future leaders.

Dr. Qubein has served as the seventh president of High Point University since 2005, leading the university through an extraordinary transformation that includes tripling enrollment, increasing the number of faculty from 108 to 280, and the construction of fifty-five new buildings on campus. Under his leadership, four academic schools have been added—Communication, Health Sciences, Art and Design, and Pharmacy. HPU's rankings moved from number seventeen to number one in Regional Colleges in the South among America's Best Colleges 2013 and 2014 by *U.S.News & World Report*. Additionally, *U.S.News & World Report* ranks HPU number one in Undergraduate Teaching in the South for 2014.

Prior to accepting his role as the president of High Point University, Dr. Qubein served as chairman of a consulting firm with clients in business and professional services. He is the recipient of many national awards, including the Cavett (known as the Oscar of professional speaking), the Horatio Alger Award for distinguished Americans, the Ellis Island Medal of Honor, the Daughters of the American Revolution's Americanism Award, and Sales and Marketing International's Ambassador of Free Enterprise. Toastmasters International named him the Top Business and Commerce Speaker and awarded him the Golden Gavel Medal. Dr. Qubein has been inducted into the Speakers Hall of Fame and Beta Gamma Sigma, the honor society for business leadership.

He served as president of the National Speakers Association, which has a membership of four thousand professionals, and is the founder of the National Speakers Association Foundation, where the Philanthropist of the Year Award is named after him.

His business experience led him to help grow a bank in 1986, and today, he serves on the board and the executive committee of BB&T, a Fortune 500 financial corporation with $185 billion in assets and 35,000 employees. Dr. Qubein is also chairman of Great Harvest Bread Company with 224 stores in forty-two states and serves on the board of La-Z-Boy Incorporated, one of the world's largest and most recognized furniture retailers. He also served as a former trustee of the YMCA of the USA, which oversees 2,600 YMCAs across the country.

Dr. Qubein has written a dozen books and recorded scores of audio and video learning programs. He is an active speaker and consultant addressing business and professional groups across North America. You can reach him at nqubein@highpoint.edu or visit his website, www.nidoqubein.com.

NICK NANTON, ESQ.

A three-time Emmy Award–winning director, producer, and filmmaker, Nick Nanton, Esq., is known as the Top Agent to Celebrity Experts around the world for his role in developing and marketing business and professional experts through personal branding, media, marketing, and public relations.

Nick serves as the CEO of the Dicks + Nanton Celebrity Branding Agency, an international branding and media agency with more than 2,200 clients in thirty-three countries. He has produced large-scale events and television shows with Steve Forbes, Brian Tracy, Jack Canfield (creator of the Chicken Soup for the Soul series), Michael E. Gerber, Tom Hopkins, Dan Kennedy, and many more.

Nick is recognized as one of the top thought leaders in the business world, speaking internationally and coauthoring thirty-four bestselling books, including the *Wall Street Journal* bestseller *Story Selling*.

Nick has been quoted in *USA Today*, the *Wall St. Journal*, *Newsweek*, *BusinessWeek, Inc.* magazine, the *New York Times*, *Entrepreneur magazine, Forbes,* and FastCompany.com. He has appeared on ABC, NBC, CBS, and FOX television affiliates around the country, as well as on E!, CNN, FOX News, CNBC, MSNBC, and hosts his own series on the Bio Channel, *Profiles of Success*.

A member of the Florida Bar, Nick is a voting member of the National Academy of Recording Arts & Sciences, a member of the National Academy of Television Arts & Sciences, and the National Academy of Best-Selling Authors. He spends his spare time working with Young Life, Downtown Credo Orlando, Entrepreneurs International, and rooting for the Florida Gators with his wife, Kristina, and their three children, Brock, Bowen, and Addison.

JW DICKS, ESQ.

JW Dicks Esq., is a *Wall Street Journal* best-selling author, Emmy Award-winning producer, publisher, board member, and advisor to organizations such as the XPRIZE, the National Academy of Best-Selling Authors, and the National Association of Experts, Writers and Speakers.

JW acts as strategic business development counsel to clients internationally and has been quoted on business and financial topics in such national media as *USA Today*, *The Wall Street Journal*, *Newsweek*, *Forbes*, CNBC.com, and *Fortune Small Business*.

Considered a thought leader and curator of information, JW has more than forty-three published business and legal books to his credit and has coauthored with such legends as Brian Tracy, Jack

Canfield, Tom Hopkins, Steve Forbes, Nido Quebin, Dr. Ivan Misner, Dan Kennedy, and Mari Smith. He is the resident branding expert for *Fast Company's* internationally syndicated blog and is the editor and publisher of *Celebrity Expert Insider*, a monthly newsletter sent to experts worldwide.

JW is called the "Expert to the Experts" and has appeared on business television shows airing on ABC, NBC, CBS, and FOX affiliates around the country. His coproduced television series, *Profiles of Success*, appears on the Bio Channel, along with other branded films he has produced. JW also coproduces and syndicates a line of franchised business television shows and received an Emmy Award as executive producer of the film, *Mi Casa Hogar*.

JW and his wife of forty-two years, Linda, have two daughters, two granddaughters, and two yorkies. He is a sixth generation Floridian and splits his time between his home in Orlando and his beach house on Florida's west coast.